THE
WILDERNESS
EXPERIENCE

LURE OF THE SEA

WRITINGS AND PHOTOGRAPHS

SELECTED AND EDITED BY

JOSEPH E. BROWN

A Harvest Original

HARCOURT BRACE & COMPANY

SAN DIEGO • NEW YORK • LONDON

A TEHABI BOOK

Requests for permission to make copies of any part of the work should be mailed to: Permissions Department, Harcourt Brace & Company, 6277 Sea Harbor Drive, Orlando, Florida 32887-6777.

Rachel Carson, "The Enduring Sea" from *The Edge of the Sea* by Rachel Carson. Copyright © 1955 by Rachel L. Carson, renewed 1983 by Roger Cheistie. Reprinted with permission by Houghton Mifflin Company, New York.

Naomi James, excerpt from *Alone Around the World*, originally titled *At One with the Sea*, by Naomi James. Copyright © 1979 by Bara Trading Company, Inc. Reprinted with permission by Hutchinson, a division of Random House, U.K., and Stanley Paul, publisher.

Hannes Lindemann, "The Big Jump" from *Alone at Sea* by Hannes Lindemann. Copyright © 1958 by Hannes Lindemann. Reprinted in its abridged form.

Jack London, excerpt from *The Cruise of the Snark* by Jack London. Copyright © 1906, 1908, 1911, and 1939. Published by The MacMillan Company, 1911.

Malcolm McConnell and Carol McConnell, excerpt from *First Crossing: A Personal Log* by Malcolm & Carol McConnell. Copyright © 1983 by Malcolm McConnell and Carol McConnell. Reprinted by permission of W. W. Norton & Company, Inc.

Gerry Spiess, "Overboard," excerpted from *Alone Against the Atlantic* by Gerry Spiess. Copyright © 1981 by Gerald F. Spiess and Marlin Bree. Reprinted by permission of the authors.

Library of Congress Cataloging-in-Publication Data

Lure of the sea: writings and photographs / selected and edited by Joseph E. Brown. — 1st ed.

    p. cm.— (The wilderness experience)

"A Harvest original."

"A Tehabi book."

ISBN 0-15-600229-9 (pbk.)

1. Voyages and travels. 2. Ocean travel. I. Brown, Joseph E.,

1929- . II. Series.

G465.L87 1996

910.4´5—dc20

96-13562

CIP

Lure of the Sea was conceived and produced by Tehabi Books. Nancy Cash–*Series Editor and Developmental Editor*; Laura Georgakakos–*Manuscript Editor;* Kathi George-*Copy Proofer;* Andy Lewis–*Art Director*; Sam Lewis–*Art Director*; Tom Lewis–*Editorial and Design Director*; Sharon Lewis–*Controller*; Chris Capen–*President*.

Illustrations by Neil Shigley

Harcourt Brace & Company and Tehabi Books, in association with The Basic Foundation, a not-for-profit organization whose primary mission is reforestation, will facilitate the planting of two trees for every one tree used in the manufacture of this book. This edition is printed on acid-free paper that meets the American National Standards Institute Z39.48 Standard.

Printed in Hong Kong through Mandarin Offset.

First edition 1996

A B C D E

CONTENTS

LURE OF THE SEA

It was the world of books that first opened my mind to the world of the sea. As a boy growing up in San Francisco, a city hugged by saltwater where sea fever comes as naturally as breathing, I became a Jack London buff at an early age. With my San Francisco Public Library card as my passport, I witnessed seal hunting off Japan thanks to the turn-of-the-century adventure author. I went oyster-pirating in London's little sloop *Razzle Dazzle* in San Francisco Bay, and weathered an Asian typhoon at London's side aboard the schooner *Sophie Sutherland,* one of London's many real life adventures that provided such gripping realism and substance to his later fiction.

Other literary sea classics only whetted my appetite for the real thing in those formative years. With Herman Melville as my guide, I chased an elusive white whale in *Moby Dick,* explored the still-unspoiled nineteenth-century South Seas in the pages of *Typee.* Robert Louis Stevenson taught me the ways of pirates, the Polish-born novelist Joseph Conrad (my parents gave me a copy of *A Conrad Argosy* on my fourteenth birthday), the romance of blue-water adventuring and the motivation of those who travel upon the oceans. Vicariously, I circled the globe with pioneer solo sailor Joshua Slocum, marveling at how he managed the feat with nothing more than a simple compass and a one-handed alarm clock for navigation. Too, I sat spellbound as Nordhoff and Hall center-staged the events that led up to the mutiny aboard the *H.M.S. Bounty,* the dispatch of her tyrannical master to the perils of the open sea, and the self-imposed exile of the mutineers—a fate worse than Captain Bligh's, as it turned out—on lonely, isolated Pitcairn Island.

But perhaps the most important "sea book" I've ever acquired and read (years later) was one by a much lesser-known author. Published in 1957, *Peter Freuchen's Book of the Seven Seas,* a concise mini-encyclopedia stemming from Danish-born Freuchen's own burning curiosity about the oceans around him—their history, the life within them, their dynamics, their treasures and mythology—catapulted me toward both a lifelong career and avocation tied to the sea.

The sea has inspired writers ever since ancient man gazed at the expanse of saltwater beyond his shores and wondered about the meaning of it all. Until he learned more about the oceans, however, before he plumbed their depths and even later was able to look down upon their imposing presence from space (an astronaut might well wonder why the planet was named "Earth" instead of "Water") the sea's might and mystery filled him as much with fear as with admiration and awe. Through history, our feelings about the sea have been ambivalent. Whereas Joseph Conrad once declared flatly that the sea "has never been friendly to man," Gertrude Ederle, the first woman to swim the English Channel, expressed an opposite feeling. "It sounds crazy, I know," she once said. "But when I swim in the sea I talk to it. I never feel alone when I'm out there."

Fear it or love it, the sea is the most dominating influence on earth. Covering 70 percent of the globe's surface, it is the great engine that drives our weather systems, provides a never-ending (but, some fear, threatened) food supply, a storehouse of minerals, a highway for transportation and, to scientists, clues to the very origin of all life on earth. The sea both separates and connects all of the world's peoples; Freuchen observed that "ripples from a pebble thrown by a child could be traced all over the Seven Seas if only we had instruments delicate enough to record them."

The sea humbles us all—being the smug, space-conquering, atom-splitting superachievers that we are. We are quickly reminded, as scholar Elizabeth Mann Borgese notes, that "human achievements shrink considerably in impressiveness and significance when one studies the ocean environment." No small-boat sailor who has ever ventured far from his safe harbor—tossed about by a storm or immobilized in the Doldrums, watching an exquisite ocean sunset or encountering a whale—would question the wisdom of that statement.

As an adult, I bought the first of four sailboats to further explore and enjoy the sea I had read about in the literary classics of my youth. I not only reread London, Melville, and Conrad, I began devouring the work of contemporary sailors who with equal eloquence and compassion had recorded their feelings about the element into which they had ventured. And in doing so, I made another happy discovery. Neither the quality nor the quantity of sea prose had diminished with the years. While Melville may have written *Moby Dick* with a quill pen, and Wayne Carpenter *The Voyage of Kristina* with a word processor, each managed to equally convey the magnificent, universal appeal of the oceans—the last, truly untamed wilderness on earth.

Perhaps the greatest challenge in being asked to edit this book was not in locating material suitable to its theme, but in making the agonizing decision of what had to be left *out.* I started with my own "sea library," a full bookcase of volumes on the sea, boats and boating collected over the years, much of it during the period I was privileged to serve as editor of *Oceans* and, later, *Sea & Pacific Skipper* magazines, both labors of love.

The growth of sea literature in recent years has been phenomenal. There are at least two book clubs devoted entirely to nautical themes, and boating subjects enjoy a small but healthy slice of the national and international magazine market. The nautical section of my local bookstore, the Owl & Turtle in Camden, Maine, is one of its most popular; in the deep freeze of winter, when local boats are tucked away for the season, it is positively *jammed.*

In my search, libraries and maritime museums in my adopted state of Maine, a state whose nautical heritage runs as deep as its winter snows, were likewise productive. Each book I pored through led to others, compounding my dilemma of choice.

In making preliminary decisions, I found myself becoming reacquainted with many old friends . . . some of whom I have never even met. Jack London had been dead and gone thirteen years when I was born in 1929, for instance, yet his words drove me ever closer to a sea destiny each time I reread them. I never met Rachel Carson, either, yet her two epic works on the sea and its shore, *The Sea Around Us* and *The Edge of the Sea* occupy a treasured niche in my home library.

It's no coincidence that with the exception of Carson's thoughtful essay, all the excerpts and essays in this book involve sailing craft rather than power vessels. I've traveled in a wide variety of motor vessels, from fishing boats to freighters and Navy warships. Although they all provided a measure of enjoyment, none offered the intimacy with the sea of a small boat moving along under wind power alone. The 27,000-ton aircraft carrier *Essex* indeed took me to sea, but it was the days aboard my *Caprice, Whisper, Gracie,* and *Snow Goose* that rewarded me with an intimate relationship with the sea, the closest thing to the feeling of oneness with the ocean environment that Gertrude Ederle must have experienced as she struggled against cold and current in her historic English Channel swim.

Nor is it a coincidence, either, that among the sailor/writers whose work is included in this book, three of them— one-third—were single-handers. They sailed not only against odds stacked against them by nature, in an environment of great loneliness, but in matters of decision making, were dependent upon their own skills and instinct. With no one else aboard to share the experience, it is the solo sailor who perhaps most of all is driven to the creative summit to describe the lure of the sea.

There are both gales and calms in the pages that follow, both anxious moments and tranquil times, stretches of empty ocean wilderness as well as quiet, snug, safe harbors at voyage's end. May this modest sample of sea literature entice, enrich, and entertain. And may you always have fair winds and following seas! —*Joseph E. Brown*

THE SEA

Combining her twin childhood interests of writing and science, Rachel Carson went on to become one of the most distinguished environmental writers of our time. Her book Silent Spring, *though fiercely attacked by the chemical industry, won wide acclaim and was credited with a ban on DDT and with creating widespread concern over ocean pollution. With a degree in marine biology, Carson summered on the Maine coast which perhaps inspired two of her finest books on the sea,* The Sea Around Us *and* The Edge of the Sea. *In this conclusion to the latter book, she contemplates the deeper meaning of the wilderness that is the world ocean. —J. E. B.*

Excerpts from *The Edge of the Sea* by

RACHEL CARSON

Now I hear the sea sounds about me; the night high tide is rising, swirling with a confused rush of waters against the rocks below my study window. Fog has come into the bay from the open sea, and it lies over water and over the land's edge seeping back into the spruces and stealing softly among the juniper and the bayberry. The restive waters, the cold wet breath of the fog, are of a world in which man is an uneasy trespasser; he punctuates the night with the complaining groan and grunt of a foghorn, sensing the power and menace of the sea.

Hearing the rising tide, I think how it is pressing also against other shores I know—rising on a southern beach where there is no fog, but a moon edging all the waves with silver and touching the wet sands with lambent sheen, and on a still more distant shore sending its streaming currents against the moonlit pinnacles and the dark caves of the coral rock.

Then in my thoughts these shores, so different in their nature and in the inhabitants they support, are made one by the unifying touch of the sea. For the differences I sense in this particular instant of time that is mine are but the differences of a moment, determined by our place in the stream of time and in the long rhythms of the sea. Once this rocky coast beneath me was a plain of

9

sand; then the sea rose and found a new shoreline. And again in some shadowy future the surf will have ground these rocks to sand and will have returned the coast to its earlier state. And so in my mind's eye these coastal forms merge and blend in a shifting, kaleidoscopic pattern in which there is no finality, no ultimate and fixed reality—earth becoming fluid as the sea itself.

On all these shores there are echoes of past and future: of the flow of time, obliterating yet containing all that has gone before; of the sea's eternal rhythms—the tides, the beat of surf, the pressing rivers of the currents—shaping, changing, dominating; of the stream of life, flowing as inexorably as any ocean current, from past to unknown future. For as the shore configuration changes in the flow of time, the pattern of life changes, never static, never quite the same from year to year. Whenever the sea builds a new coast, waves of living creatures surge against it, seeking a foothold, establishing their colonies. And so we come to perceive life as a force as tangible as any of the physical realities of the sea, a force strong and purposeful, as incapable of being crushed or diverted from its ends as the rising tide.

Contemplating the teeming life of the shore, we have an uneasy sense of the communication of some universal truth that lies just beyond our grasp. What is the message signaled by the hordes of diatoms, flashing their microscopic lights in the night sea? What truth is expressed by the legions of the barnacles, whitening the rocks with their habitations, each small creature within finding the necessities of its existence in the sweep of the surf? And what is the meaning of so tiny a being as the transparent wisp of protoplasm that is a sea lace, existing for some reason inscrutable to us—a reason that demands its presence by the trillion amid the rocks and weeds of the shore? The meaning haunts and ever eludes us, and in its very pursuit we approach the ultimate mystery of Life itself. ❧

DREAM HARBOR

Although he was not quite forty when he died in 1916, writer/sailor/adventurer Jack London blazed a meteoric literary trail during his productive lifetime: fifty-one books, hundreds of short stories, essays, and plays. He was the highest-paid, best-known writer of his era, best remembered for his gripping stories of man against nature and adventure tales of the Yukon and of the sea. In January 1907, London launched a heavily-timbered, forty-five-foot wood ketch, the Snark, *in which he hoped to cruise around the world with his wife, Charmian—a life's dream. The* Snark *provided a series of both adventures and misadventures before illness forced London to abandon both boat and dram in the South Pacific after twenty-seven months and return home to California, but not before the San Francisco–born author saved its essence for future sea buffs in his best-selling* The Cruise of the Snark, *from which the following is excerpted. —J. E. B.*

Excerpts from *The Cruise of the Snark* by

JACK LONDON

It will not be so monotonous at sea, I promised my fellow-voyagers on the *Snark*. "The sea is filled with life. It is so populous that every day something new is happening. Almost as soon as we pass through the Golden Gate and head south we'll pick up with the flying fish. We'll be having them fried for breakfast. We'll be catching bonita and dolphin, and spearing porpoises from the bowsprit. And then there are the sharks—sharks without end."

We passed through the Golden Gate and headed south. We dropped the mountains of California beneath the horizon, and daily the sun grew warmer. But there were no flying fish, no bonita and dolphin. The ocean was bereft of life. Never had I sailed on so forsaken a sea. Always, before, in the same latitudes, had I encountered flying fish.

"Never mind," I said. "Wait till we get off the coast of Southern California. Then we'll pick up the flying fish."

We came abreast of Southern California, abreast of the Peninsula of Lower California, abreast of the coast of Mexico; and there were no flying fish. Nor was there anything else. No life moved. As the days went by the absence of life became almost uncanny.

"Never mind," I said. "When we do pick up with the flying fish we'll pick up with everything else. The flying fish is the staff of life for all the other breeds. Everything will come in a bunch when we find the flying fish."

When I should have headed the *Snark* southwest for Hawaii, I still held her south. I was going to find those flying fish. Finally the time came when, if I wanted to go to Honolulu, I should have headed the *Snark* due west. Instead of which I kept her south. Not until latitude nineteen degrees did we encounter the first flying fish. He was very much alone. I saw him. Five other pairs of eager eyes scanned the sea all day, but never saw another. So sparse were the flying fish that nearly a week more elapsed before the last one on board saw his first flying fish. As for the dolphin, bonita, porpoise, and all the other hordes of life—there weren't any.

Not even a shark broke surface with his ominous dorsal fin. Bert took a dip daily under the bowsprit, hanging on to the stays and dragging his body through the water. And daily he canvassed the project of letting go and having a decent swim. I did my best to dissuade him. But with him I had lost all standing as an authority on sea life.

"If there are sharks," he demanded, "why don't they show up?"

I assured him that if he really did let go and have a swim the sharks would promptly appear. This was a bluff on my part. I didn't believe it. It lasted as a deterrent for two days. The third day the wind fell calm, and it was pretty hot. The *Snark* was moving a knot an hour. Bert dropped down under the bowsprit and let go. And now behold the perversity of things. We had sailed across 2,000 miles and more of ocean and had met with no sharks. Within five minutes after Bert finished his swim, the fin of a shark was cutting the surface in circles around the *Snark*.

There was something wrong about that shark. It bothered me. It had no right to be there in that deserted ocean. The more I thought about it, the more incomprehensible it became. But two hours after we sighted land and the mystery was cleared up. He had come to us from the land, and not from the uninhabited deep. He had presaged the landfall. He was the messenger of the land.

Twenty-seven days out from San Francisco we arrived at the island of Oahu, Territory of Hawaii. In the early morning we drifted around Diamond Head into full view of Honolulu; and then the ocean burst suddenly into life. Flying fish cleaved the air in glittering squadrons. In five minutes we saw more of them than during the whole voyage. Other fish, large ones, of various sorts, leaped into the air. There was life everywhere, on sea and shore. We could see the masts and funnels of the shipping in the harbor, the hotels and bathers along the beach at Waikiki, the smoke rising from the dwelling-houses high up on the volcanic slopes of the Punch Bowl and Tantalus. The custom-house tug was racing toward us and a big school of porpoises got under our bow and began cutting the most ridiculous capers. The port doctor's launch came charging out at us, and a big sea turtle broke the surface with his back and took a look at us. Never was there such a burgeoning of life. Strange faces were on our decks, strange voices were speaking, and copies of that very morning's newspaper, with cable reports from all the world, were thrust before our eyes. Incidentally, we read that the *Snark* and all hands had been lost at sea, and that she had been a very unseaworthy craft anyway. And while we read this information a wireless message was being received by the congressional party on the summit of Haleakala announcing the safe arrival of the *Snark*.

It was the *Snark*'s first landfall—and such a landfall! For twenty-seven days we had been on the deserted deep, and it was pretty hard to realize that there was so much life in the world. We were made dizzy by it. We could not take it all in at once. We were like awakened Rip Van Winkles, and it seemed to us that we were dreaming. On one side the azure sea lapped across the horizon into the azure sky; on the other side the sea lifted itself into great breakers of emerald that fell in a snowy smother upon a white coral beach. Beyond the beach, green plantations of sugar-cane undulated gently upward to steeper slopes, which, in turn became jagged volcanic crests, drenched with tropic showers and capped by stupendous masses of trade-wind clouds. At any rate, it was a most beautiful dream. The *Snark* turned and headed directly in toward the emerald surf, till it lifted and thundered on either hand; and on either hand, scarce a biscuit-toss away, the reef showed its long teeth, pale green and menacing.

Abruptly the land itself, in a riot of olive-greens of a thousand hues, reached out its arms and folded the *Snark* in. There was no perilous passage through the reef, no emerald surf and azure sea—nothing but a warm soft land, a motionless lagoon, and tiny beaches on which swam dark-skinned tropic children. The sea had disappeared. The *Snark*'s anchor rumbled the chain through the hawse-pipe, and we lay without movement on a "lineless, level floor." It was all so beautiful and strange that we could not accept it as real. On the chart this place was called Pearl Harbor, but we called it Dream Harbor. ❦

THAT OLD BOGEY HORN

Remembered as a shy, quiet girl, Naomi James was reared about as far from the influence of the ocean as one can get—a remote New Zealand farm. But as a young woman, all that changed. Emigrating to England, she fell in love twice, once with yachtsman Rob James, and again with the sea to which her future husband introduced her. At age twenty-nine, despite being prone to seasickness and having sailed only two years, she set out in a fifty-three-foot boat on a voyage around the world—alone. In doing so, she became the first woman to single-handedly circle the globe, at the same time eclipsing the time record of the celebrated Sir Francis Chichester. She was also the first woman to sail alone around Cape Horn, dreaded for centuries by mariners for its tumultuous seas, screaming winds, and proximity to icebergs. In this passage from Alone Around the World, *she describes her encounter, perhaps a surprising one, with "the old bogey Horn." —J. E. B.*

Excerpts from *Alone Around the World* by

NAOMI JAMES

I calculated that in terms of sailing time I was just in front of Chichester's position eleven years earlier, so there was still a chance for me to "beat him" round the Horn. However, this race was seldom uppermost in my mind—more often it was the race for survival. Chichester had met some of the worst weather of his trip rounding Cape Horn. He had gone fairly close and of course the seas are worse there because of the shelving of the seabed which creates an additional disturbance. I didn't want that happening to me and chose to give the Horn a wide berth. I preferred rather to run the risk of tangling with icebergs than to catch even a glimpse of the brooding, malignant rock that was my conception of Cape Horn.

At midnight on 14 March the starboard shrouds collapsed again. I jogged along under shortened sail until morning and then went aloft to inspect the damage. Fortunately, it wasn't too bad. Unable to get the shroud plates over the bolt as originally intended, I had linked them to the bolt with a shackle and a large steel ring. It was the steel ring, gripped by the bolt, which had suffered. The strain must have been immense, for the ring had straightened into an oblong shape before parting. I replaced it with a heavy shackle and within half an hour I was on my way again. By midday I was 500 miles from the Horn.

On 17 March (Day 191) I took enough careful sights to be sure of my position. I could only trust to luck that the error in my chronometer was remaining constant; it was a predicament that at any other time would have worried me very much, but now I simply minimized the problem and concentrated on more immediate things.

> I feel relieved to have at least one good fix, for, if the weather deteriorates I may not be able to grab another sight for days. The barometer is steady at 998 millibars, which is not too exciting but I'm keeping my fingers crossed. I can still beat Chichester if I keep up this progress.

18 March, 20:00 (Day 192)

> It's bitterly cold on deck. I dressed up intending to watch the sunset but after ten minutes came below, frozen. It's very squally and at times *Crusader* is doing seven knots with just the storm jib and deep reefed main. There is a half moon in the sky which helps. I shall be able to see where I'm going.

Early on the 19th the wind fell away completely and I managed a few hours' sleep, getting up at 2 A.M. when it suddenly blew strongly from the WSW. I kept the mainsail set until 6 A.M., then hauled it down in the increasing wind, disconnected the Sailomat and began to steer. I had planned to pass within fifteen miles to the south (windward) side of Diego Ramirez Islands which lie sixty miles to the west of Cape Horn, but didn't think I would see them unless the visibility improved. It was very cold and it rained all the time. And yet despite the misery I was not too worried about the gale, as I was keyed up for the final battle, and I felt I could tackle anything!

At 4 P.M. I wrote:

> I've steered all day. The wind shows no signs of dropping yet and visibility is still poor, but I must be past the islands by now. I am going to stay on this course until I reckon that I am well past the Horn; then I shall jibe and head for Illa Los Estados on the eastern side. I only hope the wind doesn't force me farther south and into the ice. My planned course will take me as much as fifty to sixty miles south of the Horn and that is below the ice limit for this year. The sea pattern has changed, and the waves are now much shorter and steeper which indicates shallower water. *Crusader* is bouncing around like a cork. I'm glad it's no more than just gale force.

In the late evening I jibed towards Illa Los Estados, having estimated I had finally passed Cape Horn, the focal point of all my fears and apprehensions of the previous four months. Then I went to bed at 11:30 and slept for four hours, my longest uninterrupted sleep for six months. When I woke I found myself heading south and hurriedly changed course to the north-east. Curiously enough I didn't think about icebergs, but simply concentrated on coaxing the boat along in the easterly wind and worried about the wind that was increasing rapidly.

Had I but known . . . luck was with me to an incredible degree. The icebergs must have been there all right, but I didn't see them—I didn't look!

At midmorning the wind increased so I was forced to lie-a-hull; by the afternoon the wind had backed to the SW. Then I continued steering under bare poles for the rest of the afternoon. The wind force was eight with heavy squalls, but by 8 P.M. it had moderated sufficiently for me to put up the storm jib and reconnect the self-steering. I went back to my bunk feeling very tired and absolutely no elation at having passed the Horn.

In fact as I hadn't seen the dreaded rock it might as well not have been there. I wasn't too certain where it was anyway, as I hadn't been able to take sights during the previous three days, and my courses had been so erratic that my dead-reckoning position was little more than a guess. However, I was pretty sure to be over the ice limit and that worried me considerably.

Next day my mood changed:

I'm past it. Whoopee!! More than that, I'm nearly past Estados! I had the shock of my life when I went up the mast this morning and saw its dim mountains twenty to thirty miles away. My DR after three days was about fifty miles out.

Well, nobody's perfect!

I took a sun-sight as soon as I sighted the land and confirmed it as Illa Los Estados, so I broke open a bottle of Riesling, poured a glass and hurled it at the ocean. I had conclusively rounded the old bogey Horn, and I hadn't even laid eyes on it. I may even have been asleep at the time. ⚓

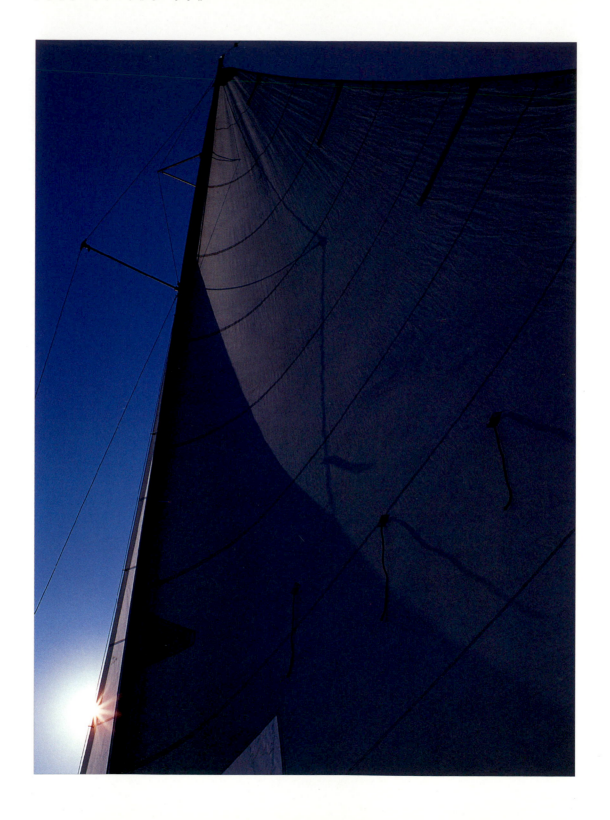

A Sneeze from Hell

When you have piled up 60,000 miles of offshore sailing, including one single-handed and three double-handed Atlantic crossings in boats from twenty to sixty feet, lived aboard several boats, and survived seventy-six days in a life raft after your boat sinks, you are bound to reflect on many faces of the ocean. Yet for Steven Callahan, presently an editor at Cruising World *magazine, there is little to exceed the joy of landfall after days or weeks at sea. In the following, Callahan describes the motivation for a sailing career and then reminisces on a particularly rewarding landfall . . . and the events leading up to it. —J. E. B.*

Landfall by

STEVEN CALLAHAN

For sixteen years I had chomped at the bit of risk-inherent ocean adventures. As a thirteen-year-old kid sprawled on the safe, dry floor of our family room, I devoured Robert Manry's book about rebuilding a thirteen-foot wooden day-sailer and voyaging across the Atlantic. My imagination was captured by images of his tight little ship, *Tinkerbell,* splashing across enormous waves. A few years later, *National Geographic* teased me with tales of Robin Lee-Graham's teenage jaunt around the globe. As I trekked to chemistry and algebra classes, I was filled with envy. For my senior project, I taught myself celestial navigation. Seven years later, my wife and I with our friend Chris became intoxicated by our first offshore passage to Bermuda. By my twenty-ninth year, I had designed and built several boats, had made my home afloat for several years, jaunted to Bermuda a half-dozen times, and felt ready for my ultimate odyssey—a dash across the Atlantic—the pond—in a small boat.

With hubris, like some kid playing God, I created my sea creature. I drew her form. Chris and I took a pile of flat lumber and began to bend it into *Napoleon Solo's* curves. We sculpted her skeleton, draped her with skin, assembled the wire rigging and aluminum bones that held her fabric wings, and painted the line that cut the water from her path. At just over twenty-one feet, *Solo* was about as roomy as a hearse, a small boat in which to tackle the Atlantic—or be buried by it. However, although I could not stand up in her, a handful of sailors had crossed the pond in lesser craft, and perhaps nearly a hundred in boats of similar size. I was not out to set records; I sought only to fulfill my childhood dreams. For these I had traded a marriage and all I owned. With nothing left to lose, and *Solo* packed with all the mementos I valued in the world, I cast off from Newport, Rhode Island, bound for England via Bermuda, 650 miles to the southeast where Chris would join me, and the Azores, 1,800 miles farther east.

From the time our wake left Bermuda behind, a substantial and smooth southwesterly swell built, gently lifting and lowering our diminutive ship from the aft quarter as we reached eastward. As our craft slid along, Chris and I traded watches, often sitting up together, our eyes sprung open with cups of thick Turkish coffee. We role-played fictional characters until our little boat was crowded with them. Chris was particularly good as an old-guard English major who waxed nostalgic about hunting lions in the Punjab, but who now sought the ultimate game: the enormous, wild, and difficult-to-track supertanker. I played the famed oceanographer Captain Clouseau of the research ship *Collapso.*

At least once each night, as if some cosmic camera was capturing our progress, a brilliant light flashed from among the stars. We could think of no rational explanation for this, nor have we ever found one. Our minds turned to the ancient mariners who returned to land with tales of unspeakable monsters and awesome mysteries.

And so it was that our adventure remained exciting and safe enough. For days we ran with the shearwaters. Unlike most land birds flapping their way about, these albatross cousins hold their long, tapered wings rigidly fixed for hours. In an endless aerobatic ballet, they soared around the wave contours, shooting skyward, wheeling, and then darting downwind at incredible speed. Their wing tips grazed so close to the water that I could detect no space between feather and sea, yet they never touched, never left a rippling trace of their oceanic existence. Our streaming, foamy wake was quickly folded into the ocean so that we, too, soon left no trace of our passing. Chris and I had become the brain of our own seabird that spread her wings, caught the wind, and flew.

Our routine was periodically punctuated by squalls. We would push until the squall was imminent, then scurry to get the canvas down before all hell broke loose—sixty knots of wind in a line squall are not unknown. Even at night it was hard to miss the brooding herds of "black cow" thunderheads with their flat, slate bottoms and roiling billows seemingly stretching into outer space. As they waltzed majestically across the sky, we watched each squall's border approach. The wind tore the sea into white caps before the rain hammered the surface into a pocked blanket of mist. Each wind line and sky shadow ran across the water and struck like a sneeze from hell, but by then we *usually* had our sails tucked away and were snugly ensconced below. After each squall blew by, we were off again, scooting eastward with the birds.

But once, when the swell turned more southerly and the barometer dipped, it became evident that a larger system—a gale—was prowling our neighborhood. We slid down the twenty-foot slopes like skiers, picking our way around moguls to boost speed and avoid bumps. We were smiles from ear to ear.

Solo's downhill surfs lengthened and quickened. The wind screamed. Ragged, savage breakers spilled everywhere. Extremely low streams of pewter cloud jetted above us, appearing almost within reach. On several downhill slides the boat began to nose into the backs of waves ahead. Any unruly breaker could roll us like dice or flip us end for end. Tight, straight lips replaced our smiles and jokes. Our minds began to dream of snug anchor lines and the smell of trees.

The blow's center seemed to alter course as the wind and waves swung increasingly to the south to smash us from abeam. Increasingly, confused seas slapped our little ship's rear so hard that she spun into the wind, her sails snapping. We hoisted the tiny storm jib and a diddly rag of mains'l and hove to, keeping the waves about fifty degrees off *Solo's* nose. In our tiny light boat, we could not keep enough canvas up to claim much victory over the windage of the hull, so it was tough to get close to the wind, but we rode the waves fine, only occasionally reeling to an angry sea that burst upon *Solo's* side with a mighty boom.

Two wave troughs came together in a crevasse that opened up like the yawning maw of Davy Jones. Our little ship fell, maybe six feet, and landed on its side with a tremendous smash. The overwhelming crest continued to roll us over. Fortunately, we were below. Chris was sitting, securely wedged at our inside control station under the main hatch, his head sticking into the jet-style Plexiglas canopy. Green water was all he could see across the hatch. I, on the other hand, had been sitting forward, navigating. First tossed against the overhead and the self-steering bracket, I then fell across the boat, landing flat against the port topsides where I was pummeled by all the navigation books that had leapt over their fiddle before dropping eight feet. If I hadn't been foolishly looking at the charts and trying to figure out what we should do if things got worse, the table would have been hinged up, completely securing the books. Luckily, all else was lashed down, including all locker tops, so we were not subject to an avalanche of chain, canned goods, or other projectiles.

Solo came upright immediately with her mast still standing and nothing missing on deck. A dribble of water through the hatch was the most to which she granted admittance. But the diabolical knockdown certainly had gained our full attention, or as full as was possible after a knock on the head. We set about inspecting every frame, every joint, every surface of the boat from bow to stern. One advantage of our twenty-one-foot boat was that we frequently saw every part of it, so problems rarely went unnoticed for any length of time. Everything was A-OK.

By the next day, the gale had blown itself out and we were left slowly roller coastering over majestic twenty-foot swells in a dying wind. Slowly the sea forgot the blow and fell flat. As we ran in light breezes, sperm whales visited us, appearing alone or in twos. Some lazily wagged by. Others joyfully breeched, landing with such great splashes that they sounded like distant thunder. I mused on what it would be like to be under one if it came down across the deck, but all the whales seemed to exude a certain sense of relaxation and play, enhancing our sense of calm and fulfillment after the storm.

Captain Clouseau, ever intent on essential oceanographic research, tossed a flip top overboard and estimated its rate of descent. It would hit bottom in three days. By then, if all went well, we would be in port in the Azores. The squalls, the gale, the whales, the depth, all imparted the immensity of our surrounds, our own pitiful insignificance. Only in port, embraced by land, would I find the audacious courage to dare spin barstool tales of how we boldly faced the sea's limitless power. We were still well offshore where there are no signposts, no guardian angels, no guarantees. My calculations showed us closing in on our target, but the sea and sky would not make it easy. As the wind strengthened, it backed to the southeast until we were close-hauled and barely making course. Our eyes strained to sight the high volcanic island of Pico. We knew we should be able to see the 7,713-foot peak from a long way off, but how far? The horizon remained a constant husky-eyed blue under distant, puffy clouds. Since ancient times, traditional Pacific navigators have so tuned their senses to the world that they can read the strength and direction of currents and the proximity of land from the mere shape of waves. Birds, sea life, cloud shapes and colors, and an encyclopedic knowledge of the stars have reliably led them to terra firma. Chris and I saw no new birds, no reflected swells, no hint of land. Apparent dark shorelines would wander to the north or south. When we were certain we had spied sloped hills, they turned into cumulus that galloped away and disappeared.

I rechecked my sextant calculations and took more sights. We were still nearly fifty miles off and perhaps too anxious to make port. Finally, a peak appeared high in the clouds, slightly darker and more angular than the puffed shadows of clouds. It remained a regular shape for an hour, two, three. . . .

All day we beat toward the volcano. Pico's raiment of clouds swept northward, revealing from the top down the breast of Mother Earth herself. The volcano had, indeed, given birth to a piece of earth upon which humans lived, labored, and loved. In her earthly arms we hoped to find rest.

That night, the heavy scent of flowers filled our nostrils. Close in to the shore we beat. The summit, in black shadow against the waxing gibbous moon, towered over us. We basked in the breeze that brought land smells and land warmth. By morning we had made our way between Pico and Faial and glided into Horta harbor from where we could gaze across the strait to the volcano rising, often into a blanket of clouds. We had been fourteen days at sea. Finally we could ease our guard, relax upon the land so still, so solid, so secure, though for days motion from the uncertain deep filled our heads, causing us to sway. It was as if the sea could not let us go, as if it wanted us never to stop. ❧

SHOOTING THE SUN

For me, the lure of the sea is not just the solace I find on the open ocean, or the adventure in riding the breath of a good wind. It is what is waiting at the end of the journey—islands. Islands are one of the rewards of sailing, and for me, what dreams are made of. They are why I am in love with the sea and with sailing. The dream of discovering an island surrounded by reefs and bays and sandy shores laden with palm and all manner of tropical vegetation, beckons the Robinson Crusoe in me. It is a lure I cannot resist.

Islands are worlds in miniature, the meeting places of sea and land, each drawing its character from the other. It is perhaps because as temporary trespassers we often fear as much as respect the sea that islands fill such a special niche in our psyches. Their draw has spawned many a novel, flamed many a romantic heart. But just what is it that accounts for this appeal? My friend Joan Tapper, editor of Islands *magazine, thinks "it's their power to remove us from the care of our daily lives. Somehow, we feel, everything is different on an island, apart from the ordinary, calmer and more creative." An island, she says, "holds out a promise—of self-sufficiency, of a new start, of a kind of paradise." And I agree with Tapper that "whether an island lives up to that promise really depends on you." For me, the promise of islands has never been broken. —J. E. B.*

Islands in My Wake by

JOSEPH E. BROWN

Mog was a middle-aged man with an infectious smile that was marred by teeth turned black by too many years of chewing beetlenut. His leathery skin was the texture of the trunks of the coconut palms his fellow islanders depended upon for their chief export trade of copra, and darkened from a lifetime as a fisherman under the broiling Micronesian sun. I didn't speak Mog's language nor he mine. But through an interpreter it became quite apparent that he was a one-man chamber of commerce for this postage stamp-sized island on which he had spent all his years. Its name now escapes memory, but the population totaled, as I recall, only nine people, a truly romantic oasis in the sea, I thought. I was wearing the uniform of the U.S. Navy, assigned to the island of Koror in the Palau archipelago. For a kid of only nineteen, away from home for the first time, these sun-splashed dots of real estate with their waving palms and glistening white sand beaches were heady stuff indeed. It was through Mog and visiting this island and its handful of people that the close relationship of man, island, and sea were driven home to me. I began to understand that of all the world's people, probably none are in closer harmony with the sea than islanders. "In these islands," Mog told me, "we tell time by the tide, not by the clock."

Mog introduced me to the thrill of traveling under sail. Although our navy ship had a motorized whaleboat, negotiating the narrow, shark-infested pass through the reef was risky. So when Mog and his fellow islanders offered to shuttle us ashore in their outriggers, our captain jumped at the chance.

Somewhere in a deep recess of Mog's ancestry lay the genesis of our sail that day. Five centuries before Christ, a small band of nomadic "Austronesians"—a polyglot strain of Caucasoid, Negroid, and Mongoloid races—set out from the Asian mainland in canoes similar to Mog's, but much larger. They first settled what is now Australia, then moved farther afield into the waters of present-day Polynesia and Micronesia. Considering the unknowns of what lay beyond the safe confines of their then-known world, they had to have been superb seamen as well as intrepid adventurers. Watching Mog maneuver his outrigger as if born to it, it was obvious that those skills were never lost through dozens of generations.

Mog dispatched four of his canoes to our ship for the ride to the beach. I'll never forget the excitement of those few minutes, first sailing and then paddling across the unbelievably beautiful Technicolor reef passing beneath us. So low lay our outrigger, I could dangle my fingertips in the sea as we sped along, almost touching the uplifted coral heads.

The next day, Mog showed us how he had taught his grandson, a boy of about three, the ways of island life and how to use instead of fear the watery wilderness that stretched to the limitless horizon.

Mog rowed the boy just beyond the surf line and then ordered him to leave the boat and float in the sea, on his back. The youngster was nervous at first, treading water furiously. But as his grandfather reassured him with a stream of chatter, he soon relaxed in the salty buoyancy of the sea. After a while, the boy no longer had to kick his feet or paddle his hands to remain afloat. It was as if for this brief moment of time, he had become *part* of the sea itself.

I've left a lot of islands in my wake since my days in Micronesia, but the memory of Mog and that first island has never left me. And no matter how many islands I've traveled to since, and there have been many, nothing can compare with arriving in one's own boat, no matter how small.

I finally had that opportunity one spring day in the early 1970s in California while I was living in San Diego. The boat was a wood sloop named *Whisper* and the island was South Coronado. It was the Coronado landfall that taught me something else about islands: if you're ever in doubt over how to find one, put some trust in nature.

Owned by Mexico, the Coronado Islands (there are two of them plus a rock) are only about seventeen miles south-west of San Diego. That's a short three- or four-hour day sail. But the day my wife Anne and I headed there for the first time, a nightmarish fog closed in on *Whisper* only a few miles past Point Loma. The boat was new to us and so was our compass, in whose accuracy I had absolutely no faith. We were, in a word, lost.

Suddenly, only a few yards away, a flock of brown pelicans soared past us in the fog, headed in the same direction as *Whisper.* "We're okay," I said to Anne, confidently. "It's pelican nesting time in the Coronados. Those birds are going home." As more pelicans flew by, we corrected our course to follow them, and hit our target dead on. Mog's lesson to his grandson so many years ago had come back to me.

By the early 1980s, another boat and another island came into our lives. The boat was *Gracie,* a traditional thirty-six-foot wood yawl. The island was Guadalupe, 180 miles off the coast of Baja California. Unlike the Coronados, which are secured to a continental footing, Guadalupe is a true oceanic island; I noted on my nautical chart that at one spot 13,000 feet of saltwater would lie under our keel on the trip out from the mainland. It is a desolate, rocky, sometimes forbidding place, far out of shipping lanes, not the kind of island you visit on the way to someplace else. Its population is about seventy—a few fishermen and their families, a small Mexican navy detachment, and six meteorologists who man a weather station.

Guadalupe was the kind of island that piqued our sense of adventure. We set sail with great anticipation. Having no electronic aids aboard *Gracie,* and no pelicans this time to guide us, we navigated instead as sailors had in generations past, "shooting" the sun, moon, stars, and planets with a sextant.

It took us forty-nine hours to make the passage from Mexico. Except for mountainous open ocean swells the first night, it was uneventful. Well, *almost* uneventful. There was a moment of near-panic when Anne sought "Lovely," our seagoing tabby cat companion of eighteen years, and couldn't find her. We feared she'd disappeared overboard until a search discovered her scrunched into a hideaway almost smaller than her body.

The morning of our Guadalupe landfall seemed almost scripted: a placid sea, a warm sun that bathed the island in soft pastels, and a pod of about forty porpoises that formed a frolicking, chattering welcoming committee.

Once anchored, a Mexican boarding party motored out in an outboard-powered *panga* to check the customs and immigration papers we had received at Ensenada. I asked one of them how many pleasure boats like ours called at Guadalupe. "I've been stationed here six months," he replied, "and you are the first one." *Ah, the perfect island getaway.*

For three days we swam, snorkeled, read paperbacks, snoozed, tramped the island's rocky trails, dived for abalone, and swapped some of our canned goods with the locals for homemade salsa and so much *langusta*—broiled, baked, stuffed in tortillas—that we reluctantly had to turn down free offers of more.

For those three days, we heard no airplanes, automobiles, or urban din, only the crashing of surf, the cries of gulls, and the murmur of wind. At our small oasis in the midst of the ocean wilderness, we had found a secure if brief moment of total peace.

As an island addict, it was inevitable that my life would eventually lead me, after a lifetime in California, to the state of Maine. Its coast is an island addict's ultimate fix: more than 3,000 islands large and small, a few of them inhabited, most of them not. That's more islands than in all the Caribbean or all of Polynesia.

When Anne and I sold *Gracie* and moved to Maine, we promised each other that the old yawl had been our last boat. But that was before we spent a week aboard the charter schooner *Timberwind,* wandering among the islands. It was a glorious week. A throwback to a bygone era, *Timberwind* was sailing at its purest. With no engine and a wood stove for cooking, we moved from island to island on a schedule dictated not by the clock, but by wind and current.

Our vow to end our island-hopping days vanished that week with the subsequent purchase of our fourth boat, a wood sloop we named *Snow Goose* which had been launched forty-four years earlier, fittingly, on an island—Maine's Mount Desert.

Every summer, we sailed *Snow Goose* to the nearby islands of Vinalhaven, North Haven, and Isle au Haut, as well as to mainland fishing harbors where life has changed little in a century. But one island constantly tempted and eluded us. It was Matinicus, a mere grayish lump on the eastern horizon when viewed from the mainland coast. It was a landfall so close—only seventeen miles—yet one seemingly so far away.

Maine's outermost inhabited island, Matinicus squats on the very edge of the Atlantic, sheltering the eastern edge of Penobscot Bay from giant swells born in Portugal thousands of miles away. What distinguishes Matinicus from its neighboring islands is its reputation for nasty, ship-threatening fog, frequent gales, heavy swells off the Atlantic, bone-numbing ice, and enough hazards such as granite shoals to gray the hair of the most experienced mariner. Records show that more than fifty vessels have met their doom in these waters since the eighteenth century.

We were fortunate the August day we sailed *Snow Goose* to Matinicus for the first time. It was a fogless, almost windless morning with a perfect, gentle wind. On the way from Rockport, a minke whale almost the size of our boat swam past, then dived out of sight. Once we were in the island harbor, snug and secure, we felt as the *Bounty* mutineers must have felt their first day on Pitcairn. That night, the crashing of the Atlantic on Matinicus's shore hummed a soothing lullaby.

Today, even as I write, the memories of those many seagoing adventures stir within me. And though *Snow Goose* is bundled up for the winter, come spring, when the first green buds appear on the birches, and the sap of the maples begins to flow, we'll ready the old girl once again and set sail for our next island paradise. ❧

One Against the Sea

In a boat hardly larger than a bathtub, a Minnesota schoolteacher named Gerry Spiess set off from Chesapeake Bay one day in 1979 to accomplish the seemingly impossible—sailing 3,800 miles across the Atlantic Ocean to England. He went alone, of course; his ten-foot-long, plywood Yankee Girl, *launched after seven years of planning and construction, was too cramped for one adventurer, let alone one or more crew. It took Spiess fifty-four arduous days to make the crossing, days of loneliness, storms and the relentless pounding of waves. But succeed he did. His account of the venture,* Alone Against the Atlantic, *is an absorbing testimonial of one man's courage and determination in facing the most challenging wilderness on earth. But was Spiess really alone? Not if you accept the "friend" he refers to in this account, the imagined companion that many single-handers have written about since the first solo sailor ventured to sea. —J. E. B.*

From *Alone Against the Atlantic* by

GERRY SPIESS

Slowly the storm was dying. Though waves were still racing along at speeds of up to twenty knots, they were now only six to ten feet high and were no longer breaking. After days of shrieking and howling around us, the wind has dropped to a more tolerable twenty knots—and, perversely, swung around to the northwest.

Yankee Girl bobbed downwind with the gray-green rollers. We were moving—an inch at a time, but moving nevertheless.

It was June 15, the fifteenth day of my voyage. Seven days of unbelievably severe weather had left me both mentally and physically drained. I was tired and dirty and miserable. Although I knew that conditions were beginning to improve, I was overcome with frustration.

I peered out a porthole for what seemed like the hundredth time that morning. An eerie white haze hung in the air, and the sun was a luminous slit on the horizon. Heaped up by the shifting wind, swiftly rolling waves heaved and boiled along the ocean's surface.

With growing impatience, I slid open the wooden hatch. I had suffered this storm long enough; I wanted to do some sailing!

As I stuck my head out the hatch, I breathed deeply and smiled for the first time in days. The fresh salt air filled my lungs and sharpened my senses. It felt wonderful to escape from the oppressive, clammy cabin, to feel like a sailor again instead of a mole.

But when I tried to stand up in the hatch, my smile quickly changed to a grimace. My muscles and tendons had been cramped and squeezed for so long that they simply wouldn't function. For a while all I could do was to kneel with my upper body sticking out of the hatchway and my arms braced on the rails. Then, gradually and painfully, I straightened my back and held my body erect at last.

I would have to take my foul-weather gear off soon. My buttocks were chafed raw, the fungus on my groin itched horribly, and I felt slimy everywhere beneath my clothing. That could wait, though. More than anything, I wanted to get the boat going. I knew that the wind would allow me to carry some canvas, but the speed and height of the waves still intimidated me. I would have to be careful.

As I stretched and looked around at the foredeck, I was relieved to see that the sails were still secure. The two jibs lay furled and strapped down under shock cords, hanked to the forestays with brass snaps. They had withstood the breaking waves and clawing winds—as I had hoped they would. The mainsail, held tightly with shock cord against the boom, seemed to have survived intact, along with the spars and rigging.

In order to hoist the jib, I first had to go forward to the bow, unhook the jibsnap, and release the shock cords. Then I would be able to pull on the halyard and raise the already reefed sail.

Cautiously I climbed out of the hatchway, grabbed the stainless-steel shroud with one hand and the mast with the other, and finally stood upright on the cabin top.

"It's a little like being on a trampoline during an earthquake, isn't it?" my imaginary friend asked mischievously.

"With a 400-pound wrestler jumping up and down on the other end," I answered, grinning.

I spread my feet apart on the hatch cover, thankful for the security of my safety harness and its three-eights-inch dacron lifeline. It had been seven long days since I'd been able to see beyond *Yankee Girl*'s immediate vicinity, and I relished the view.

"Too bad there's nothing to see but waves," my friend gibed.

"When I get tired of them, I'll let you know," I shot back.

Just standing on top of the boat filled me with elation. It was like coming out of a year—no, make that *ten* years of solitary confinement. I could breathe again!

I paused for a few seconds to plan my next move. Hoisting the jib would be tricky. *Yankee Girl*'s tiny bow didn't have much buoyancy; she would bury her nose in the water when pressed by my weight. I would have to be very careful of my footing—and work fast.

With every muscle tensed and ready to go, I waited for the right moment—a lull between the waves.

Then, over my shoulder, I saw something that made me freeze in terror.

A massive wall of water was roaring toward us. A new northwest wave—a rogue—was crossing over the old system, flattening the other waves as if they had been made of paper. I hung on to the rigging and stared.

Suddenly I realized that the hatch was still open. Foolishly, I had forgotten to close it when I'd climbed above. Now the wave was towering over it, threatening to fill *Yankee Girl*'s cabin.

Frantically I leaned backward with all my weight, hoping to lever the stern up.

The wave slammed into the transom, lifted the stern, and threw it sideways. Water raced to meet me as I clung to the shroud. For the second time since the beginning of my journey, we were capsizing!

I was plunged into the churning water. Gasping for breath, I watched, horror-struck, as the deck went completely under on the port side. Meanwhile the wave curled menacingly toward the open hatch.

Yankee Girl was now so far down that I could see inside her cabin. If she went any further, or if she were struck by another wave, she could roll all the way over. Then my safety line would wrap itself around her—and I would be trapped below the surface.

Kicking desperately, I struggled against my water-filled clothing. I clenched my hands around the stainless-steel shroud and felt its cold bite.

Then, abruptly, *Yankee Girl* righted herself—pulling me up with her.

Once again my little girl had saved me from my own carelessness.

Everything had happened so quickly that I'd been in the sea for only a few seconds. Luckily, I hadn't even lost my glasses. I didn't hesitate. With water pouring out of my foul-weather gear, I scrambled below and slammed the hatch shut behind me. I slumped on my berth, thoroughly shaken and furious with myself.

Again and again I pounded my fist into the seat cushion. How could I have been so stupid? How could I have made such an idiotic mistake? I should have known better than to have my weight up so high in conditions like these!

While I'd been standing on top of the cabin, feeling as if I owned the world, I had taken a chance—a dumb, unforgivable chance that had nearly cost me my life. I sat there for a long time, raging at myself.

Finally I became aware of my soggy clothing—and my pain. My raw, infected skin, which had been irritated by its unexpected saltwater bath, burned as if it were on fire. The tiny cabin was again full of seawater, and as the waves rolled us about the salt was literally rubbing into my wounds.

In a black mood, I rummaged around up forward until I found what I was looking for: a clean shirt and a pair of tan work pants. I stripped off my wet clothing and patted myself dry with a towel. Then I dusted talcum powder over my inflamed skin to reduce the chafing.

My pants hung loosely around my waist. In my fifteen days at sea I had lost about ten pounds.

There was no way I could wash or dry my old clothes, so I threw them overboard, knowing that they would eventually disintegrate.

I felt better after I'd dried myself off and changed my clothes, but I stayed inside the cabin anyway. I vowed that I wouldn't go above again until the next morning; I had to prove that I was still capable of disciplining myself. Besides, I needed time to think about the blunder I'd made—and learn what I could from it.

Outside, the weather steadily improved.

* * *

The next morning dawned breezy but sunny. Overnight the wind had swung to the north-northeast—perfect for a beam reach to the east. Best of all, the waves had settled down to heights of between four and five feet. Compared to the monsters that had battered us during the storm, they seemed like ripples on a pond.

Still unnerved by my unexpected dunking of the day before, I went forward to hoist the reefed jib. As I hauled in the sheets, I drew in *Yankee Girl*'s sails to the taut curves that would power her effortlessly along. With an exhilarating surge, she sliced through the water.

For the first time in eight days we were sailing a course for England.

"Looks like your luck is changing, Ger," my imaginary friend remarked.

"We'll make it yet, old buddy," I replied. ❧

PERIL IN THE MIST

Almost being run down at night in the open sea by a large ship is a recurring nightmare of any small-boat sailor. Almost being run down twice in the same voyage makes one believe in jinxes and star-crossed living. Collision didn't happen to Malcolm and Carol McConnell, but the chilling memory of the razor-thin what-might-have-been lingers yet. Both journalists, the McConnells sailed their thirty-foot sloop Matata 7,600 miles from New York to Greece. They recalled the high moments and low of the trip (such as the two encounters with ocean-going behemoths) in their delightful and inspiring cruising journal, First Crossing. *—J. E. B.*

Excerpts from *First Crossing: A Personal Log* by

MALCOLM AND CAROL MCCONNELL

The white blast of light cut into and splintered whatever weird dream was gripping me. Again when I sat up I reached instinctively to the right to cuff silent the bedside alarm clock. Instead, I banged my elbow painfully on the wooden edge of the upper berth. My legs were over the side of the bunk, still wrapped in the sleeping bag. I could feel the boat turning hard to port, the engine thudding loudly at high revs. What the hell was that light?

Again, the hot beam cut down into the cabin. Jesus, Carol was shining the nine-volt searchlight down here. I was suddenly at the companionway, the sleeping bag behind me on the cabin sole. Remembering that I was naked, I dashed back to grab my Levi's from above my bunk. The engine seemed to be racing, revved much too high, as if the throttle were stuck and the machine was going to rip itself loose from its mounts.

Stumbling up to the dew-slick cockpit, I found an even stranger scene than earlier. Carol was standing, the tiller jammed between her knees, her two arms raised above her as if in prayer to some heathen idol, the beam-gun light blasting a hot shaft of light onto the mainsail. The engine was indeed running at high revs; behind us in the moonlight, I could see a curling, bubbling wake. I shook my head hard to clear away the clotted sleep. The big genoa was backed, twanging on the shrouds as we spun in our emergency-power circle.

"What the hell . . ." I began. But something in Carol's wide-eyed expression made me stop speaking and look forward.

There was a blue and white freighter out there, *right* out there off the bow, coming dead at us, maybe half a mile away. I could see both his green and red running lights and also the creamy white bow wave curling back from his stern.

Without further speculation, my brain took over my body and I leaned down to ease the throttle. Roughly, but without anger, I pushed the beam gun away from my face and grabbed the metal handle. Then I had the tiller in my other hand and Carol was sitting down in the companionway.

"The mast floodlight," I said, my voice surprisingly calm, hiding the confusion inside. "Start flashing the floodlight and don't stop till I tell you."

She was gone inside within three seconds. The seal-beam floodlight on the forward midmast flashed on and off, billowing the genoa with bright light. I closed my eyes for a second, then grabbed a look at the dim orange disc of the compass. The freighter was coming from about 105 degrees; we were swinging hard to port, moving up on due north. So be it. We'd steer 360 degrees and hope he'd pass astern of us. That left the ship hidden by the genny, but making another turn would waste too much time. I reached down with my big toe and advanced the throttle a few more revs. We might blow some oil past the rings and loosen the stern gland, but an extra half-knot was worth the risk. Like Carol, I gripped the tiller with my knees and used both hands to flash the beam gun's hot light on the mainsail.

The boat bounded ahead; the engine thudded and roared, and we careened north through the calm water, our sails spreading the light.

When I looked aft, the freighter was just behind us, thumping away at a course perpendicular to ours. I could clearly see the details of his hull, tall derricks, and superstructure. There were white life-raft canisters stacked like supermarket fruit on his bridge deck. On his stack, a faint yellow light illuminated his company logo, some kind of squiggle inside a triangle. His engines twanged across the 400 yards of water like monstrous rubber bands. I swallowed hard, then wiped my damp palms on the legs of my jeans. If we hadn't turned, he would have nailed us.

"Kill the light," I yelled down so that Carol could hear me over the roar of our diesel.

The hot floodlight went dead, and its afterglow blanketed the water out ahead of my eyes like moonlit gauze. Bending to ease the throttle, the stack gas of the freighter washed over me, stinking like a bus station. When I stood back up, Carol was sitting next to me, staring back at the freighter's stern.

"He never even saw us," she whispered.

I released a stale breath and sat down beside her, holding the tiller stiffly before me. "Where did he come from?" I tried to keep any trace of residual anger out of my voice. We'd just had a near miss, and there was no sense trying to blame anyone for it.

She pointed off to starboard. "All I know," she said in the same tired tone, "is that one minute there was a ship going west, south of us"—she twirled her fingers toward the darkness—"and the next minute the ship was right on top of us . . . " She shook her head. "That's when I called you."

I patted her leg. Beneath her jeans, her muscles were tense. Somehow, we'd slipped south of our chartered track and into the westbound shipping lane. Either that, or more than one freighter had strayed north of the lane. I eased the throttle even more and began a slow swing to starboard, back to our original course. As we turned, I suddenly realized what had happened. Current, of course . . . a south-going current had set in with the evening flood tide. With the northerly component of the breeze behind the current flow, we'd made perhaps three or four miles of southern leeway. It was obvious to me now, an elemental piloting problem I'd completely ignored in my hedonistic longing for uninterrupted sleep.

This sure as hell won't do, I thought bitterly. On our first night at sea I'd let the boat drift south right into one of the world's most crowded shipping lanes. Foolishness, inexcusable incompetence, compounded by a bad attitude. That certainly was not the way to make it safely across the Atlantic Ocean on a small boat. Now there was no sense giving in to crippling remorse. I must simply take corrective action.

First, I had to get that blinding blanket of the worthless genoa down and furled so that we could see what was out there. Then, I'd steer north for maybe forty-five minutes and snatch a couple of radio-compass bearings to figure out just exactly where we were. After that, I would steer the boat on a safe eastward course until dawn. That was a good four hours away, and what I proposed precluded any sleep. But my body was aching for sleep—silent, mindless oblivion in that warm sleeping bag down below. I rubbed my face violently. No.

I'd sleep in the morning; now I needed my wits. For a moment, I thought of going down below and washing my face with cold fresh water from the ice chest. Then I remembered that fresh water was too precious a commodity to waste washing one's face. There was a small supply of amphetamine tablets in the medicine box . . . maybe half a tablet now. No. Ridiculous. Speed was the last thing I needed; I was nervous and strung-out enough already. What I did need now was some resolve, some strength of character. Four hours was not a terribly long time to steer a boat. Besides, we could split it up, each taking the helm an hour at a time, while the other rested on the free cockpit cushion or just inside on the comfortable quarter berth.

Standing up to look ahead, I could see the line of westbound ships on the horizon. "Take the tiller," I said. "I'm going to put some clothes on and see if I can get an RDF fix."

Carol looked uncertainly around her at the white lights of the ships moving silently through the black water. "We should have waited to leave until just before dawn, like we planned to do," she said, "so that we'd have the worst of the shipping in daylight."

"We should have done a lot of things differently," I shot back, the submerged edge of exhausted anger just breaking the surface of my voice. I caught my tone and tried to relax. "We'll take turns steering, Honey. I'll make some coffee. It'll be light in a few hours."

Carol looked around again. The moon was getting high, and the water shimmered in patches like dirty ice on a winter highway. The robotlike displays of ships' lights moved along through the rippling darkness like esoteric training aids in some computerized navigation simulator. "I didn't think it would look like this," Carol finally said in a small, disappointed voice.

I nodded in silent agreement. "Yeah . . . I know." Before ducking down to the cabin, I turned to face her again. "Don't worry, by this time tomorrow we'll be on our own."

Again Carol glanced around her. "I sure hope so." ⁕

SEA SPIRIT

One day in 1955, Hannes Lindemann of Germany left the coastal town of Harper in the Canary Islands, bound west across the Atlantic Ocean in one of the strangest craft ever to make the passage. Named Liberia II, *it was a twenty-three-and-a-half-foot long dugout canoe only twenty-nine-and-nine-tenths inches wide, patterned after native African canoes he had seen in Morocco where he had practiced medicine on a U.S. Air Force base. So odd-looking was Lindemann's ocean-spanner that Portuguese officials, required to describe it but having no idea how, settled on "a crate of secondhand goods." Lindemann later recalled his incredible voyage of hardship and exultation in a book,* Alone at Sea, *from which this is excerpted.* —J. E. B.

Excerpts from *Alone at Sea* by

HANNES LINDEMANN

On the eleventh day, with a slight wind behind me and the aid of the Canary current, I made my entrance into the tropics. Petrels and shearwaters flew listlessly over the interminable high swell from the north; they appear to need wind as much as a sailboat does, for without it they tire easily. They seemed as melancholy as I in a calm.

Small fish paid short visits to my dugout. On the fourteenth day, the first shark swam toward me; he loitered around the *Liberia* beating a steady tattoo with his tail fin against the cork pads on the side of the boat. I found that all sharks were curious when the boat moved slowly. Dolphins hunted their small victims and at times shot right out of the water in their eagerness. I threw them tidbits, and they rushed at them greedily only to turn away disappointed when they found they were not meat. Dolphins are confirmed carnivores, active day and night in their hunt for meat. During the night I could hear the hard beating of bird wings in the darkness. Before the moon rose, dolphins trailed long gray-white trains of bioluminescence through the water. Sometimes the canoe or the rudder touched a jellyfish or some other plankton form which lit up briefly and darkened again at once. Twice at night I caught glimpses of a dragonfly and a butterfly in the beam of my flashlight. Unfortunately, they did not have the presence of mind to take refuge on my canoe.

Every night now I was delighted by a display of shooting stars. On the sixteenth day a shearwater deposited its droppings in front of my bow and that night a comet swung down from the skies. Were they omens of good luck?

Throughout the long, dark nights I watched, entranced by the bioluminescence in the waters around me. Not enough has been written about this phenomenon of the sea, about the light the inhabitants of the sea make for themselves: for they are afraid of the rays of our sun and make their own sunshine. At night they turn themselves into spirits through the dark in a profusion of shapes and forms: spotlights, strip lights, and floodlights are an old story to marine creatures. Tail-lights, halos, headlights are their natural inheritance. Nor is that all: plankton forms let other forms glow and shimmer for them; they catch bacteria which will light up at their command, or they grasp at lighted bacteria and bask in its rays. Jelly-fish ornament their billowing skirts with shining bacteria and swim like ballerinas through the wet darkness. The fewer the stars that shine at night, the more friendly the light of the sea. Sometimes I found the nocturnal world of the ocean hard to fathom, but its very mystery lent enchantment to my lonely nights.

One night, as I watched the shimmering plankton, I thought I should like to taste it, at least once. It is, after all, the basic food of the sea. I hung out a net of the finest mesh, which had the effect of a sea anchor and made the boat groan over her additional burden. Because of this I left the net out for only an hour and then drew it up to examine my catch. Lighting my flashlight to investigate, I saw some sort of repellent vermin moving at the bottom. After a moment of hesitation, I took a spoonful and nibbled carefully. Immediately my mouth was full of an intense burning sensation. Scooping up a cup of sea water, I rinsed my mouth, and then smeared my lips with heavy cream; but the burning continued for hours. Since then, I have not fished for plankton—although I think it was not plankton that burned, but floating poisonous tentacles from a Portuguese man-of-war caught in the net. . . .

I watched a dolphin investigate a tentacle field; it hunted a fish that had taken refuge there and appeared to be immune to the stinging streamers. Not so the dolphin, who was burned, and quickly retreated from the field. I would not give one cent for the life of an underwater swimmer caught in a bed of these burning tentacles. I have often been stung by little pieces of these streamers that the surf has torn from the parent body and that have lodged on a coral reef; it feels like boiling tar poured on the skin, and even picric acid applied at once does not alleviate the pain.

After two weeks the ocean was still so calm that I could see, deep in the water, a swarm of dolphins mingling with their pilot fish. The shrouds had rusted and streaked the sail a pale yellow, so I decided to wrap them in sailing yarn. I was standing on the deck, working on this project, when I heard a loud splash before the bow and saw dolphins swimming for cover to the *Liberia.* My eye was caught by the passing shadow of a large fish. Another time, a periscope broke the flat surface, perhaps the arm of an octopus or the head of a turtle. It happened fast, and when I came closer, the periscope was discreetly submerged. The sea was alive; gelatinous masses floated everywhere, mixed with plankton and the excrement of whales. Only the trade winds had died.

I had to wait for my sixteenth day for a change. On that day heavy cloud banks approached from the north, followed by the longed-for wind. Shearwaters took a new lease on life, playing in the water like children and running lightly over the waves on their yellow feet until they were drawn into the air by the wind. Their cry resembled a goat's bleat rather than the song of a bird, and they did not charm me so much as the smaller stormy petrels; but they had the advantage of keeping me busy for a long time trying to classify them. Finally, after checking carefully in *Birds of the Ocean* by Alexander, I decided that my companions were the Mediterranean shearwaters, *Puffinus kuhli,* the largest Atlantic shearwater. Although they stayed near the *Liberia,* they showed no curiosity about her, seldom bothering to turn around and look at her. I did not find it easy to classify shearwaters and petrels from my small boat; if I had had weapons, I could have shot them and made accurate identifications then and there. Instead, I took color pictures and made my identification later.

Now the trade winds blew as they are reputed to, and I sailed westward. Squalls rushed over the sea and forced me to concentrate on handling the boat. I no longer saw much sea life; a few swarms of flying fish leaped into the air, fleeing dolphins, the sea birds became livelier, but plankton and water striders disappeared into the rough seas.

On the eighteenth day, the wind veered to the northwest—often a danger signal—clouds and sea merged and the horizon drew threateningly close. Crests of white foam capped the surface as the old trade winds and the winds of the new storm met and battled for control of the waves. At first the *Liberia* stuck obstinately to the old wave course, but with the help of my paddle I forced her into line. Moments such as these, when two wind directions meet head on with full power, can be extremely dangerous for small boats. I was relieved when the new winds took control of the waves and they became regular. Later that afternoon, the tornado—as squalls are sometimes called on the West African coast—had passed and the trade winds blew again. I was happy to see them despite the acute discomfort they caused. Whenever they blew with any degree of strength, I was wet—water dripped off my beard and ran down my neck, my sunglasses were blurred, and my drenched clothes clung to my body. The continual wet increased the soreness of my buttocks, which burned so intensely that I could hardly bear to put any weight on them.

On that same day—my eighteenth—I threw overboard the last of my oranges and apples; they had all rotted. Up to now the fruit had supplied me with all the liquid I needed. I was never thirsty and my intestines functioned beautifully. After the fruit ran out, I switched to a daily liquid intake of fourteen ounces of evaporated milk and a mixture of one and a half pints of mineral water and a bit less than a half pint of red wine, which I kept cool in a canteen wrapped in wet cloth. The raw onion I ate every day constituted my vitamin intake, and it was evidently enough, for I developed no symptoms of scurvy, such as bleeding gums, throughout the entire voyage. . . .

During my days of calms I had sailed through a sea that resembled bouillabaisse from Marseilles or a soup of fish eggs. Now that the trade winds blew, the soup had greasy waves. There were times when I grew alarmed at the violence with which the dugout rolled and lurched in the turbulent ocean. On the whole, however, I felt secure; my new rudder was strong, and the heavy following seas could do no real damage. . . .

For two more days the wind blew with strength, and then on the twenty-sixth day it veered, first to the east, shortly thereafter to the southeast, and finally to the south. Soon the wind died, and the waves, subjects of the kingdom of the winds, flattened—only the ever-present high Atlantic swell remained. ⁊⟨

Rites of Passage

Wayne Carpenter has ventured into the Atlantic twice in small boats, both times with his wife Kristina and two daughters, Lisa and Jennifer. The first trip was aboard a thirty-three-foot sloop, Marie Rose; *the second voyage, which Carpenter described in a delightful book,* The Voyage of Kristina, *was in a twenty-seven-foot sloop which the Carpenters had finished building from a bare hull in Cardiff, California. In the following, Carpenter distills the essence of those two experiences, particularly what the sea taught the Carpenter family in terms of togetherness and a shaping of life's goals. The former editor of* Rudder *and* Pacific Skipper *magazines, Carpenter was a newspaper reporter and financial writer before a discovery of the sea swept him away to new pursuits. He presently lives and writes in Arnold, Maryland, near Annapolis. —J. E. B.*

A Family Afloat by

WAYNE CARPENTER

She was a gentle, almost timid little girl and remained somewhat so even as she grew into adulthood. Yet our firstborn daughter, Lisa, in later years would do things that would scare the hell out of me, such as make a February passage offshore from Connecticut to Florida with her husband, Richard, and apparently think it not all that unusual.

Our second daughter, Jennifer, was quite different from her sister. Somewhat outspoken (pushy, her mother says), she was, in fact, quite measured when taking risk. I don't think she would have made the midwinter passages Lisa made. Instead, she has been riding around the world on a bicycle with her husband, Bob, and is somewhere in Bali even as this is written. She has been on this trip for more than two years, been through India and Malaysia and most of Europe. After returning home, I suspect eventually she will settle in some remote place such as the mountains of West Virginia or the open spaces of Wyoming or Montana.

For many, it would appear the girls are taking crazy risks with their lives, but they were raised with taking risks, measured and calculated risks, risks in which the odds were clearly stacked in their favor and in which the rewards were more than worth the possible dangers. For them, the pablum of total security and safety is not a life, but a mere existence, and of all the great and wonderful lessons the sea offered our daughters, this was among the most important.

We had been a family of four, a mom and dad and two preteen daughters, and we were, without question, the antithesis of what one would envision when one thought of adventure on the high seas. The likes of the great single-handed sailors such as Joshua Slocum, Vito Dumas, or that of my personal sailing hero, John Guzzwell, we were not, and it was almost a shock to most when we would pull into port for the first time, particularly after an obviously long passage. They simply could not believe that such a young family could have sailed such distances without additional help, but we did, first for about three years in a wooden thirty-three-foot ketch built in France in 1958, then for another three years in a twenty-seven-foot sloop that was partially built by us in 1977. Each boat, in various ways, was superior to the other and each was loved dearly by us, for they not only were our transportation, but our safety and home in an environment in which we clearly were not meant to live. The sea, I am convinced, merely tolerated our trespassing, and would, from time to time, swat us around a bit to remind us exactly who and what we were and exactly who was boss out there.

"Why are you doing this?" our friends and family would ask as we prepared for the trip the first time. "You know this is crazy. You have two precious little girls to worry about."

I had many, many answers, at the time, but not one could fully explain exactly what caused us to quit good jobs and sell everything. The drive was equally strong in my wife, Kristina too, for she never would have agreed to adventure aboard a sailboat if it were not. Complicating the situation was a scene from an old Cary Grant movie that would flash before me each time the question was asked. It takes place at the end of the film as Grant is about to get on an airplane to once again run from all responsibility and/or seek adventure in some new glamorous and exciting part of the world, depending on one's point of view. "There's a whole world out there," he tells his teary-eyed grown daughter, a product of one of his earlier world jaunts and whom he met only a few days earlier, "and I've just begun to see it! Come with me," he implores her. Alas, she cannot, as someone must watch over the real world. Grant looks at her a little sadly, but only for an instant, then turns on his heel and bounds off to board the airline, ostensibly never to be heard from again.

It was hard to not think of myself as the irresponsible Grant when people would ask that question. Sometimes it seemed that the only difference between Grant's character and me was that while he roamed the world alone, I was taking my wife and two daughters along. Then one day the answer became clear and I knew why and it was simple: I had to know what was on the other side. I had to know how people lived and talked and ate and drank, but more than that, I wanted to share those experiences with my family. I learned a long time ago that nothing was much fun if I could not share the experience, if not give it. The sea would be our highway. We could take our beds with us, stay as long as we chose, then set sail for another adventure.

The lessons of the sea, though, would be among our most important, for the sea truly taught us the meaning of life. The sea taught us how important our own lives were by showing us how unimportant we were in the grand scheme of things: it could survive just fine without us, thank you kindly, regardless of what we thought of ourselves. This was not lost on Lisa and Jennifer, in spite of their young ages, and has contributed mightily to their becoming the successful women they are today.

More than debatable philosophical insights, though, the sea taught Lisa and Jennifer the true worth of education. If children in school studied how to draw angles in geometry classes, our girls saw those angles drawn a half dozen times a day and drawn with purpose. Incorrectly drawn and we could be shipwrecked. They took that seriously. So did I. They saw and understood how the angle was taken from the face of the earth and a bearing of the sun and how an azimuth and back azimuth worked to show us exactly where we were. They learned that there was no room for an error in addition or subtraction here and that sometimes it was necessary to do things over and over again until one was certain it was done correctly. They learned how to determine where our little ship was headed and how to get there by working with the laws of the sea rather than fighting them, which they quickly found to be impossible to do most of the time in any event. Most important, in addition to the teamwork with the sea and the rest of us, each girl learned how to rely on herself, that if she did not know the rules of the sea, the consequences could be serious indeed, far worse than going a weekend without TV. The education of sitting on a deck alone in the middle of the night watching billions of stars that can only be seen in such darkness, the introspection afforded at those times, the wonderful long hours of conversation, real conversation, these were the wonderful things we received, but on which no educational value can be placed.

Cruising families were not unknown in the late sixties and early seventies, but they were unusual enough that not much information about how to travel by boat with children was available. We read everything we could, but the knowledge was quite inadequate and often decades old. In retrospect, I find that while seemingly a hindrance, this lack of information was ultimately a blessing, for it allowed us to discover certain things on our own, the most surprising of which was just how much Kristina and I actually needed the help of our daughters on our sailing adventure.

This discovery came in 1974 on our first crossing of the Atlantic, which also was our first major crossing of any kind. Understandably nervous, Kristina was unable to sleep for the first several nights. Every lurch of the boat, every groan of a plank, every slap of a halyard portended to her a disintegrating vessel that was surely going to sink at any moment, and kept her from the sleep she was desperately beginning to need. Then, in a few hours, it would be time for her to take the watch again, only to be followed by another period of off-watch sleeplessness. Finally, out of desperation, I pressed the girls into taking watches, first for thirty minutes at a time with one of us keeping them company, then for thirty minutes alone. Slowly they were weaned into taking full two-hour watches when the weather was calm. Eventually Kristina was able to relax enough to sleep soundly and for a period long enough to be of some benefit. In the beginning, we both felt guilty about having the girls stand watches. After making landfall at the Azores, however, we realized that *Mom and Dad* had not sailed across the Atlantic, but that *we* had sailed across the Atlantic, and it was a genuine and honest team effort. On that first crossing, we truly needed the help of those little girls, who were then only ten and eleven years old, and they knew it, and from that moment on, they would never be the same. They had undergone certain rites of passage, and in the most literal sense of the phrase at that.

Little by little Kristina and I ceased being the parental authority figures and were replaced, to a large extent, by that greatest of all parental figures, Mother Nature. Her tolerance for having things done later was nonexistent, as was her intolerance for not doing things right the first time. As parents, Kristina and I loved Mother Nature. We turned her into our disciplinarian. The girls also were aware that their parents didn't argue with Mother Nature either. She was completely indiscriminate.

Though these ideas often were difficult to explain, I think our various foreign hosts both admired and understood the concept of familial teamwork on a small boat. It is a concept that seems rare in American families today. For Lisa and Jennifer, though, making them a genuine part of the sailing team, an honest part of the crew and not just deck scrubbers and dish washers, was to give them a sense of true worth within the family unit. I imagine it was a feeling similar to that of earlier eras when families were forced to work together in order to survive. Sailing together taught us that standing totally alone was not always the way things should be done, even though it was a popular way to think.

People we met would light up when we explained that concept to them, and we nearly always did, because the most common question we were asked the world over was the equivalent of, "But what about your daughters' education?" On a more pragmatic level, we taught the girls, in the early years, from a correspondence course. It was a course developed for the children of diplomats and it was excellent. And in this school, there was no pressure to be passed on to a succeeding grade level simply because the calendar said so. They remained in the fifth and sixth grades until the course was finished and completely understood. That happened to take nearly two years. Interestingly enough, they were promoted two grade levels during a period at home between voyages. Even then, they did not find their schoolwork intellectually challenging.

The girls were in high school during our second three-and-a-half-year voyage, and this time the problem of education was considerably more difficult. There were no acceptable commercial courses available, so we ended up inventing our own curriculum, which we structured around the Three Rs. Social studies, natural science, and geography were no problem, for those classes were a part of our everyday life. Kristina's talent lay in logic and math, so she taught math. I taught writing and instructed the girls to write weekly letters that I would be allowed to read describing their adventures to friends. The reading assignments were great fun, for I assigned only best-selling novels with historical themes. *The Winds of War, The Diary of Anne Frank,* and *On The Beach* taught World War II history and showed what war could be like in the nuclear age. *The Good Earth* and *Tai Pan* provided an introduction to Asian culture. And early European history was taught through the writings of authors such as Anya Seaton. It wasn't long before a threat of depriving the girls of their books, even in jest, was to threaten to punish them severely indeed.

Often we would invent courses. If there was a doctor on board in a port, we would shamelessly corner him or her into giving a lecture on life science or biology. A German couple we sailed in company with for several months gave the girls personalized German lessons as well as a few courses in drawing and painting. However, one of the most interesting courses was that of business education. It was in the U.S. Virgin Islands that Jennifer and I set up shop as street vendors and sold trinkets to tourists for fun and profit. We both got great educations from that experience, and Jennifer, in particular, learned she could make very good money on her own if she was willing to take risk. And of course, we toured on land every chance we got, from the Citadel in Halifax, to Simón Bolívar's home in Caracas.

More than simply sailing for long periods over oceans, though, we had the privilege of rare and exciting experiences. One winter in Canada, we installed a wood-burning stove on our boat and then proceeded to let cold lock our boat in ice for the duration. And for more than two years, we sailed without benefit of electricity or engine. I would gamble to say there are not many alive in this world today who have sailed across an ocean without modern conveniences. We lit kerosene running lights every night and steered by the gentle yellow glow of a kerosene anchor light, and we read books by candlelight. No engine also meant we had to sit totally becalmed in the middle of the Atlantic Ocean for five days. It was tedious at times and frustrating. But it taught us patience and was totally necessary if one was ever to know the exhilarating thrill and power a gentle breeze could bring to one's life once it did finally materialize.

Primitive and inconvenient? Yes. Educational? Perhaps. Personally enhancing? Absolutely. We consider all those experiences a rare privilege.

Whether visiting a popular port where people were accustomed to the comings and goings of cruising boats or some isolated island village, our reception almost always was the same. It was warm and friendly and nearly instant. The reason, I believe, was that sailboat or no sailboat, everyone everywhere recognized two little girls, a mother, and a father as that international icon known as a family. A family was imminently identifiable, approachable, and above all, safe. To fuss over one's child was a normal and usual way to pay a high compliment to the parents. It was the international language of saying, "Hello and welcome to our land and we are glad you are here and would like to get to know you better." We in turn would fuss over their children or some object of beauty or praise the land and indicate how very pleased we were to have the privilege of just being there. Social barriers and fears melted under such conditions and warm and beautiful friendships that were to last for days and years to come were formed. The fact that we arrived by sailboat made it all that much more of a novelty.

Being able to outfit and provision a small boat for a voyage to just about any place in the world filled us all with the self-confidence and pride to know we could, with relative ease, get through some of the chores and problems that seemed so insurmountable at home. I think we all learned that to face an empty ocean with a small boat ultimately was to confront the wilderness of one's own mind, to search and explore and eventually, to blaze a trail through the extraneous clutter of our modern society to a more reasonable and comforting way of life, not comforting in the material sense, but more importantly, in the spiritual sense. ❧

Daniel Allisy, Carlo Borlenghi, R. Brisius, Christian Fevrier, Federico Fiorillo, G. Lhote, and **Gilles Martin-Raget** represent the very best of European sea and sailing photographers. Their combined work spans five America's Cup competitions, three Admiral's Cup races, two Whitbread Round the World races and a dozen multihull Grand Prix and Transoceanic races. They have worked as staff photographers for publications throughout Europe and the United States, and their photographs have been featured often in magazines, books, and exhibits worldwide.

PAGE i—Storm at sea. (Fevrier)
PAGE 6—Seadog. (Borlenghi)
PAGE 7—Sunlight on water. (Borlenghi)
PAGE 11—Shell on sand. (Borlenghi)
PAGE 22—Anchored under palm and sky. (Martin-Raget)
PAGE 25—Port at sunset. (Borlenghi)
PAGE 26—Under sail under clouds. (Allisy)
PAGE 32—Waves. (Lhote)
PAGE 33—Cape Horn. (Allisy)
PAGE 41—Forty-knot gale. (Fevrier)
PAGE 42–43—Aboard the *Brooksfield*. (Brisius)
PAGE 45—Sea and sky. (Fevrier)
PAGE 65—Wind on water. (Borlenghi)
PAGE 66–67—Wave off bow. (Brisius)
PAGE 68—Bad weather. (Borlenghi)
PAGE 76—Fifty-knot gale. (Fevrier)
PAGE 78—Sailboat through spray. (Borlenghi)
PAGE 87—Clouds over sea. (Fiorillo)
PAGE 97—Anchored off rocky shore. (Borlenghi)
PAGE 99—Sailboat in mist. (Allisy)

Gary Braasch has photographed major environmental assignments for *LIFE, Audubon, Discover, Natural History,* and the *New York Times* magazine, and has been published in more than 100 magazines worldwide. His photography has appeared in five books and has exhibited much of his work. Braasch is an active campaigner and contributor to conservation efforts throughout the world. He lives in Nehalem, Oregon.

PAGE ii–iii—Sailboat at sea.
PAGE 4—Harbor ropes.
PAGE 5—Boats at sunset.
PAGE 24—Boats in afternoon.
PAGE 36—Dawn. Playa del Carmen.
PAGE 44—Sailing. Columbia River.
PAGE 56—Afternoon sail.
PAGE 70—Evening sail.
PAGE 83—Ocean patterns.

Willard Clay is a former botany professor whose well-known photographs have captured the splendor of much of the United States. Using a large 4x5 format exclusively, he produces razor-sharp images of nature at its finest. His work has appeared in such publications as *Arizona Highways, Smithsonian, Reader's Digest,* and *National Geographic.* His book credits include *Yellowstone: Land of Fire and Ice* and *Grand Teton: Citadels of Stone.* Clay lives in Ottawa, Illinois.

PAGE 8—Sunset. The Gulf of Mexico.
PAGE 12–13—Surf and rocky shore. Acadia N.P.
PAGE 55—Rolling Island. Acadia N.P.

Kathleen Norris Cook is well known for her outstanding images of outdoor subjects, primarily of the western United States. For three consecutive years her work has been selected for display in Kodak's prestigious Professional Photographer's Showcase in the Epcot Center Pavilion. The recipient of numerous awards, Cook has completed two of her own books, *Exploring Mountain Highways* and *The Million Dollar Highway,* and has contributed to a number of other magazines and books, including *On the Trail of the Desert Wildflower and Women in Wilderness.* Cook makes her home in Colorado.

COVER—Seascape at Thunder Hole. Acadia N.P.
PAGE 58–59—Twilight with sailboat.
PAGE 69—Tidal detail. Acadia N.P.

Jeff Foott has worked as a cinematographer and still photographer since 1970. He specializes in wildlife and landscape photography and is dedicated to environmental protection. Formerly are searcher in marine biology, a national park ranger in Yosemite, a mountain climbing guide, and ski patrol member, Foott now documents wild animals and landscapes in national parks and other wild places. His work has appeared in virtually every major wildlife and nature publication, including *Audubon, National Geographic, Smithsonian,* and *Natural History.* Foott resides in Jackson, Wyoming.

PAGE14—Sunlight on ocean's ripples.
PAGE 30–31—Tracy Arm. Southeast Alaska.
PAGE 35—Killer whale. Johnstone Strait.
PAGE 86—Humpback whale breeching. Baja.

Bob Grieser is one of the country's great yachting photographers and a widely respected photojournalist. A former White House photographer for the *Washington Star* newspaper and chief photographer of *Chesapeake Bay* magazine, Grieser is chief photographer for the San Diego bureau of the *Los Angeles Times.* His yachting photos have been featured in traveling exhibits and in numerous publications including *Yachting* and *Sailing* magazines, and in his book *Chesapeake Bay.* His coverage of two America's Cup competitions was widely reproduced and was featured in the books *America's Cup 1851 to 1992* and *America's Cup 1995.* Grieser lives with his wife, Georgia, in San Diego.

PAGE iv—Sailboat at sea.
PAGE viii—Boat in full sail.
PAGE 15—Sunset sail.
PAGE 16—Sunset. Fiji.
PAGE 20–21—Sunlight through clouds over sea.
PAGE 46–47—Bad weather sail.
PAGE 50—Cruising classic.
PAGE 57—Crab on rock.
PAGE 75—Sole Sailer.
PAGE 77—Fogbank.
PAGE 84–85—Pelicans over sea as fog rolls in.
PAGE 88—Sunset chat.
PAGE 96—Cliffs at sunset.
PAGE 98—Sailing into the sunset.

JC Leacock is a large-format photographer whose images capture the beauty, grandeur, and intimacy of the American landscape. His work has appeared in such publications as *Sierra, Wilderness, Outside,* and in Audubon calendars, among others. His upcoming book, *Colorado Close-Up* will be released in March 1997. Leacock lives in the mountain town of Nederland, Colorado.

PAGE 95—Sailing on the schooner *Shearwater.*

Tom and Pat Leeson have been photographing wild places and wildlife as a husband-and-wife team for over twenty years. From their home base in Vancouver, Washington, the Leesons have worked on assignment for the National Geographic Society and National Wildlife Federation, as well as supplying images to *Time, LIFE, Reader's Digest,* Nike, Inc., and American Airlines. Besides photographing two award-winning books on the American bald eagle, their images have appeared in such books as *On the Trail of the Desert Wildflower, Canyons of Color: Utah's Slickrock Wildlands,* and *Yellowstone: Land of Fire and Ice.*

PAGE 23—Strait of Juan de Fuca.
PAGE 48—Black-browed albatross.
PAGE 94—Cape pigeon.

Connie Toops is a naturalist and freelance photojournalist whose images have appeared in the Audubon Society and Sierra Club calendars, in leading naturalist magazines, in books published by the National Geographic Society, the National Wildlife Federation, Sierra Club, and others, including *Women in Wilderness.* Her own books include *National Seashores, Everglades,* and *Great Smoky Mountains.* Toops makes her home in the Smoky Mountains of West Virginia.

PAGE 34—Sun on sails.
PAGE 49—Sunrise. Mississippi Sound.
PAGE 60—Sailing dinghy. Mississippi Sound.